Contents

Introduction

The use of matting and layering in card making can change a card out of all recognition and for the extra expense of some pieces of paper or card, you can change a basic card into a treasure that someone will keep forever.

I always make sure I have a good stock of plain card in the variety of colours I know I enjoy using and add in some mirror card, some glittery cardstock and something with a nice pearly sheen – and I have my 'craft arsenal' ready and waiting.

If I choose to use a crafting CD then more often than not the right backing paper is waiting right there for me and I can mix and match to my heart's content.

Double-sided tape is often my choice of adhesive but if you struggle with getting your layers straight, try a clear photo glue that allows the paper or card to be repositioned. Whether you use a paper guillotine or trimmer, scissors or a craft knife, simple cutting and layering can be the rock you build your card on to that makes sure it will be a real star!

Damask Rose

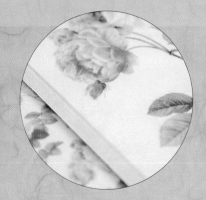

Materials:
A4 sheet of pearly baby pink card

A5 sheet of linen finish silver card

Extra piece of baby pink pearl card

A4 sheet of rose backing paper
and Damask Rose topper from
Cardmaker's Year CD

Tools:
Bone folder

Double-sided tape

Guillotine

2mm ($^1/_8$in) foam tape

Tweezers

Instructions:

1 Fold the A4 sheet of pink card in half and crease heavily with a bone folder. Alternatively use a scoring board to fold the card.

2 Cut the silver card down to a smaller size that will leave about a 6mm (¼in) border of pink card showing and attach to the pink card with double-sided tape or glue.

3 Cut out the Damask Rose topper and then cut a spare piece of baby pink card slightly larger than the topper.

4 Cut the A4 sheet of rose backing paper down in size so that you again have a 6mm (¼in) or so border of silver around it and fix it on to the card.

5 Finally stick the topper on to the piece of baby pink card and then fix that to the main card using foam tape to give the card extra dimension.

Gold and Roses

*Here the same Damask Rose topper has been paired with a darker burgundy
cardstock and the paler option on the CD of white roses backing paper.*

Happy Geishas

Materials:

A4 sheet of white card

A5 sheet of almond blossom paper

A4 sheet of characters backing paper and Happy Geisha topper from Tales of the Orient CD

Apple blossom stamp on cream card, watercoloured and cut out

Craft sticker butterfly on acetate

Two craft jewels

Tools:

Bone folder

Double-sided tape

Guillotine

Tweezers

Silicone glue

Instructions:

1 Fold the A4 sheet of white card in half and crease it heavily with a bone folder. Alternatively use a scoring board to fold the card.

2 Cut the characters backing paper down to a smaller size that will leave about a 5mm (³/₁₆in) border of white card showing and attach to the white card with double-sided tape or glue.

3 Cut out the Happy Geisha topper.

4 Cut the A4 sheet of almond blossom backing paper down in size so that you again have a 5mm (³/₁₆in) or so border of characters paper around it and fix it on to the card.

5 Stick the topper on to the card and then attach the stamped blossom image with silicone glue. Attach the craft sticker butterfly which has been stuck on acetate and cut out. Finally attach the craft jewels.

Geishas on Green

Here the same Happy Geisha topper has been layered with black cardstock and some Japanese maple leaf design paper from the CD and finally some stamped bonsai trees that have been produced on shrink plastic.

Portrait of a Lady

Materials:

A4 sheet of cream card

A5 sheet of gold mirror card

A5 sheet of black pearl card

A4 sheet of purple fabric backing paper and Lady topper from Victorian Companion CD

Stamped image of oval frame, decorative bow and embellishments (on cream card, stamped in Patina Gold embossing powder and dried with a heat gun)

Tools:

Bone folder

Double-sided tape

Guillotine

Silicone glue

Tweezers

Craft knife

Heat gun

Instructions:

1 Fold the A4 sheet of cream card in half and crease heavily with a bone folder. Alternatively use a scoring board to fold the card. Then trim down to a squarer shape on the guillotine.

2 Cut the black card down to a smaller size that will leave about a 6mm (¼in) border of cream card showing and attach the black card with double-sided tape or glue.

3 Cut out the Lady topper and then the oval frame and bow. Attach the Lady portrait to the back of the frame using double-sided tape.

4 Cut the gold mirror card down in size so that you have a 6mm (¼in) or so border of black around it, and fix it on to the card. Trim the purple fabric paper to leave a 6mm (¼in) gold border and attach it to the card.

5 Stick the lady in the oval frame on to the card with silicone glue and then fix the bow and embellishments using silicone as well.

Lady on Black

Here the same framed lady is displayed on a much smaller, plainer card with no patterned backing paper – just the cream, gold and black card.

Lazy Daisies

Materials:

A4 sheet of white card

A5 sheet of burgundy card

Two sheets co-ordinating Art
  Nouveau Flowers papers

Four paper daisies

Large craft sticker butterfly
  stuck on acetate

Tools:

Bone folder

Double-sided tape

Guillotine

Silicone glue

Tweezers

Photo glue

Instructions:

1 Fold the A4 sheet of white card in half
and crease heavily with a bone folder. Alternatively use
a scoring board to fold the card. Then trim down to a square on
the guillotine.

2 Cut the burgundy card down to a smaller size that will leave about a 6mm (¼in) border of
white card showing and attach the burgundy card with double-sided tape or glue.

3 Cut out four 60 x 60mm (2³/₈ x 2³/₈in) squares, two in each of the Art Nouveau Flowers
papers and attach them to the burgundy card as shown. I use photo glue to attach these as
you can slide and position them for quite a few minutes before the glue dries.

4 Cut four small 30 x 30mm (1¹/₈ x 1¹/₈in) squares, two in burgundy and two in white card and
attach them diamond-wise to the papers.

5 Finally stick the daisies and the butterfly on to the card using a little silicone glue.

Daisy Trio

Here the same daisies are displayed on a taller, simpler card using just some warm marbled papers with a touch of gold.

Dancing with Shadows

Materials:

A4 sheet of white card

A5 sheet of pale yellow glitter card

A4 sheet of black and white silhouette backing paper and Dancing topper from Dancing with Shadows CD

Cream organza ribbon

Tools:

Bone folder

Double-sided tape

Guillotine

Silicone glue

Tweezers

Instructions:

1 Fold the A4 sheet of white card in half and crease heavily with a bone folder. Alternatively use a scoring board to fold the card.

2 Cut the glitter card down to a smaller size that will leave about a 6mm (¼in) border of white card showing and attach to the white card with double-sided tape.

3 Cut out the Dancing topper.

4 Trim the A4 sheet of black and white silhouette paper to give a 6mm (¼in) glitter border and attach to the card with double-sided tape and glue. I use both as glitter card is notorious for not letting things stick permanently to it and I find this combination works well.

5 Stick the topper on to the card and attach an organza bow using silicone glue.

Shades of Grey

Here the same topper is cut out in decreasing sizes and layered with silicone glue. This card also features silver card and a charcoal grey backing paper.

Mistletoe Child

Materials:

A4 sheet of green card

A5 sheet of green card

A4 sheet of misty holly backing
paper and Mistletoe Child topper
from Enchanted Christmas CD

Plastic holly and berries

Bright red organza ribbon

5mm ($3/16$in) nib gold calligraphy
felt tip pen

Tools:

Bone folder

Double-sided tape

Guillotine

Silicone glue

Tweezers

2mm ($1/8$in) foam tape

Instructions:

1 Fold the A4 sheet of green card in half
and crease heavily with a bone folder.
Alternatively use a scoring
board to fold the card.

2 Cut the misty holly paper
down to a smaller size that
will leave about a 6mm
(¼in) border of green card
showing. Before you attach
it to the card, swipe the gold
pen along the edge to give a
gold border. Do this also on
the main card.

3 Cut out the Mistletoe Child
topper and then cut the A5
piece of green card down so
that the topper can sit on it with
a 5mm ($3/16$in) border all round.
Attach the topper using double-
sided tape. Use the gold pen on
the edges of this smaller green
card too.

4 Using foam tape, stick the
smaller green card with the topper
on it on to the card, towards the
bottom right-hand corner.

5 Arrange the holly leaves and
organza bow at the top left and
attach them using silicone glue.

Christmas Cutie

Here the same Mistletoe Child is arranged on a brighter
backing and a double green ribbon is added to the side.

Beautiful Bonsai

Materials:

A4 sheet of black card

A5 sheet of purple mirror card

A4 sheet each of purple characters
backing paper and green Japanese
maple leaves from the Tales of the
Orient CD

Stamped image of bonsai tree and
coin on cream card stamped with
verdigris powder

Twinkling H20 paints

3mm (⅛in) self-adhesive pearls

Tools:

Bone folder

Double-sided tape

Guillotine

Tweezers

2mm (⅛in) foam tape

Instructions:

1 Fold the A4 sheet of black card in half and crease heavily with a bone folder. Alternatively use a scoring board to fold the card.

2 Cut the purple character paper down to leave a narrow black border and then cut the green maple leaf paper down to leave a narrow purple character paper border. Stick both to the card.

3 Stamp and then emboss the bonsai image and colour it with the paints.

4 Cut the purple mirror card a little larger than the bonsai tree card and attach it with double-sided tape. Then attach this topper to the main card with foam tape to add some height.

5 Add the self-adhesive pearls and then using the foam tape add the tassel and stamped coin.

Purple Bonsai
Here the bonsai tree is left plainer and matted and layered on a much darker choice of background.

Holly Christmas

Materials:

A4 sheet of cream card

A5 sheet of gold mirror
  card

A5 piece of calligraphy card

A4 sheet of decoupage
  images with frame for
  Holly Christmas

Tools:

Bone folder

Double-sided tape

Guillotine

Silicone glue

2mm ($1/_8$in) foam tape

Tweezers

Craft knife and cutting mat

Decoupage snips

Instructions:

1 Fold the A4 sheet of cream card in half and crease heavily with a bone folder.
Alternatively use a scoring board to fold the card.

2 Cut the gold card down to a smaller size that will leave about a 6mm (¼in) border of
cream card showing and attach it with double-sided tape or glue.

3 Cut the calligraphy paper to allow a 3mm ($1/_8$in) gold border and then attach that to
the card using foam tape.

4 Cut all the pieces needed for the 3D decoupage from the sheet, including the
frame, using a craft knife and cutting mat or decoupage snips.

5 Slowly assemble the decoupaged picture starting with the biggest piece, then
stick the frame over the top. Finally layer up the other smaller pieces, using plenty of
silicone glue.

Tartan Greetings
The same decoupage design looks very different when displayed against
a red and green tartan background with some gold craft sticker corners.

Cattleya Orchid

Materials:

A4 sheet of white card

A5 sheet of lilac pastel lace backing paper

A5 piece of lilac pearl card

A4 sheet of 3D decoupage paper with Cattleya orchid design

Lilac organza ribbon and rhinestone buckle

Tools:

Bone folder

Double-sided tape

Guillotine

2mm (1/8in) foam tape

Silicone glue

Tweezers

Decoupage snips

Craft knife and cutting mat

Instructions:

1 Fold the A4 sheet of white card in half and crease heavily with a bone folder. Alternatively, use a scoring board to fold the card. Then trim down to a slightly squarer shape on the guillotine.

2 Cut the pastel lace paper down to the height of the white card and using the decoupage snips (or a small pair of scissors) follow the line of the lace to cut a wavy edge each side. Attach to the main card using double-sided tape.

3 Cut out the decoupage images and trim the lilac pearl card to a size a little larger than the main image to give a 3mm (¹/₈in) border all round. Attach the main image to the lilac pearl card.

4 Attach the main image and lilac pearl card to the card using the foam tape. Then build up the decoupage using silicone glue.

5 Thread some lilac organza ribbon through the rhinestone buckle and attach to the top left of the topper, using foam tape.

Art Nouveau Orchid

Here the same orchid decoupage is framed with a darker Art Nouveau patterned paper and embellished with a brown tassel and ribbon.

Friends

Materials:

A4 sheet of cream card

A4 sheet of gold mirror card

A5 piece of blue marbled backing paper

A4 sheet of 3D decoupage paper with Kate Greenaway Friends design

Tools:

Bone folder

Double-sided tape

Guillotine

Silicone glue

Tweezers

Decoupage snips

Craft knife

Instructions:

1 Fold the A4 sheet of cream card in half and crease heavily with a bone folder. Alternatively use a scoring board to fold the card.

2 Cut the gold mirror card so you have a piece that gives a border of roughly 6mm (¼in) all round of cream card, then attach it using double-sided tape. Cut a second piece of gold card to the same width and height as the oval on the decoupage sheet and attach that as well.

3 Cut out the decoupage images.

4 Attach the main picture to the gold card and build up the decoupage using silicone glue.

William Morris Friends

Here the same Kate Greenaway decoupage is framed with a darker William Morris patterned paper and some corners have been added from the decoupage sheet.

White Poinsettias

Materials:

A4 sheet of black card

A4 sheet of blue mirror card

A5 sheets of charcoal and blue paisley papers

Spray of white poinsettia flowers with glittery leaves and baubles

Tools:

Bone folder

Double-sided tape

Guillotine

2mm ($^1/_8$in) foam tape

Silicone glue

Tweezers

Instructions:

1 Fold the A4 sheet of black card in half and crease heavily with a bone folder. Alternatively use a scoring board to fold the card.

2 Cut the blue mirror card down to a smaller size and the charcoal grey paisley paper smaller again and layer on to the black card.

3 Cut another piece of blue mirror paper and a slightly smaller piece of blue paisley paper and layer those – this time using the foam tape to add another dimension to the card.

4 Add a small rectangle of blue mirror card and then attach the spray of white poinsettias using silicone glue.

Vintage Poinsettias

This time the spray of white poinsettias is displayed on turquoise glitter card and some vintage Christmas backing paper.

Oriental Cherry Tree

Materials:

A4 sheet of burgundy card

A4 sheet of bordered backing paper from Tales of the Orient CD

Oriental Cherry Tree topper from Tales of the Orient CD

Burgundy organza ribbon

Tools:

Bone folder

Double-sided tape

Guillotine

Tweezers

Japanese screw punch

Instructions:

1 Fold the A4 sheet of burgundy card in half and crease heavily with a bone folder. Alternatively use a scoring board to fold the card.

2 Trim the A4 backing paper (available on the CD right next to the topper) and fold it right around the card without sticking it down.

3 Open the card. Holding both layers steady, punch two holes in the left-hand side of the front, about 25mm (1in) or so so apart.

4 Using the tweezers, thread a small piece of burgundy ribbon down through one hole and up through the other. Repeat once or twice so that the ribbon is firmly attached with a tail of around 25mm (1in) coming from each hole.

5 Cut out the topper and attach to the card with double-sided tape.

Cherry Blossom
Here the cherry tree design is used with two different backing papers attached with a diagonal craft sticker to disguise the join.

Egyptian Market

Materials:

A4 sheet of cream card

A4 sheet of orange toned backing
paper, beige hieroglyphics paper
and Egyptian Marketplace topper
all from the Egyptian Adventure CD

A5 piece of gold mirror card

Tools:

Bone folder

Double-sided tape

Guillotine

Tweezers

Instructions:

1 Fold the A4 sheet of cream card in half and crease heavily with a bone
folder. Alternatively use a scoring board to fold the card. Open the card and
trim the front in half lengthwise.

2 Cut the orange backing paper down to a smaller size and attach to the
inner face of the card leaving a border all the way round.

3 Cut a piece of the beige hieroglyphic paper to sit on the narrow front flap
of the card, leaving a border the same width as in step 2.

4 Cut out the topper and layer it on to a piece of gold mirror card.

5 Attach the layered topper to the front flap of the card using double-sided
tape on the upper part of the topper only.

Egyptian Adventure

The Egyptian Marketplace is displayed here with a sandy papyrus paper and a darker backing, also available on the Egyptian Adventure CD.

Butterfly and Roses

Materials:

A4 sheet of cream card plus
  small extra piece

A4 sheet of heavyweight acetate

A5 piece of gold mirror card

A5 sheet of carnation
  backing paper

Selection of pressed roses,
  leaves and alyssum

Three jewel brads and a
  die-cut butterfly

Tools:

Bone folder

Double-sided tape

Guillotine

Photo glue

Tweezers

Japanese hole punch

Instructions:

1 Fold the A4 sheet of cream card in half and crease heavily with a bone folder. Alternatively use a scoring board to fold the card.

2 Cut the gold card slightly smaller than the main cream card and then the carnation paper smaller again. Attach them with double-sided tape.

3 Fix the extra piece of cream card with double-sided tape and start arranging the flowers and leaves.

4 Once you are happy with the flower arrangement, stick the flowers and leaves down using a little photo glue or another clear glue.

5 Fold the acetate over the card. Open the card and using the Japanese screw punch, make three holes on the left-hand side of the front. Fix the brads in the holes to hold acetate and card together.

6 Finally attach the die-cut butterfly to the outside of the card with a little glue.

Bows and Roses

Here the pressed roses are displayed with lacy backing papers and the acetate is held on with small organza bows.

Hearts and Flowers

Materials:

A4 sheet of white card

A4 sheet of lilac pearl card

A5 sheet of oriental butterfly paper

A4 sheet heavyweight acetate

Stamped and embossed
  parchment heart-shaped doily

Assortment of pressed flowers
  and leaves

Pearl brads

Tools:

Bone folder

Double-sided tape

Guillotine

Photo glue

Tweezers

Japanese screw punch

Instructions:

1 Fold the A4 sheet of white card in half and
crease heavily with a bone folder. Alternatively use a scoring board to fold the card.
Trim the card down to a square on the guillotine.

2 Cut the lilac pearl card down to a smaller size and the butterfly paper smaller still
and layer on to the white card, leaving a narrow border between each layer.

3 Attach the small square of lilac card in a diamond position and add the stamped and
embossed heart at a slight angle.

4 Arrange the pressed flowers and once you are happy, attach them with photo glue.

5 Trim the acetate to the size of the larger lilac card piece and place it on top. Open
the card and use the Japanese screw punch to make holes through the corners of the
acetate and the front of the card. Fix the brads in place to secure the acetate.

New Baby Girl

Here the same pressed flower arrangement is made into a new baby card for a little girl.

Fairy Silhouettes

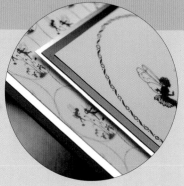

Materials:

A4 sheet of black card

A4 sheet of gold mirror card

A4 sheet of fairy silhouette
backing paper and
topper from Dancing with
Shadows CD

Tools:

Bone folder

Double-sided tape

Guillotine

2mm ($^{1}/_{8}$in) foam tape

Tweezers

Instructions:

1 Fold the A4 sheet of
black card in half and
crease heavily with a
bone folder. Alternatively
use a scoring board to
fold the card.

2 Cut the gold card slightly
smaller to leave a border,
and the backing paper
slightly smaller still, and
attach to the card with double-
sided tape.

3 Cut a piece of gold card
slightly larger than the topper
and attach the topper to it,
leaving a narrow border.

4 Attach the topper to the main
card using the foam tape to add a
little lift to the card.

Flower Fairies

*Here the fairies are surrounded by a purple and lilac
backing paper and some lilac organza ribbon.*

A Beautiful Hat

Materials:

A4 sheet of white card plus a little extra

A5 sheet of apricot backing paper

A4 sheet of backing paper and Beautiful Hat topper from Fashion Boutique CD

Apricot organza ribbon and satin rosebud

Tools:

Bone folder

Double-sided tape

Guillotine

Silicone glue

Tweezers

Instructions:

1 Fold the A4 sheet of white card in half and crease heavily with a bone folder. Alternatively use a scoring board to fold the card. Then trim down to a slightly squarer shape on the guillotine.

2 Trim down the apricot backing paper to slightly smaller than the card, and then trim down the backing paper that matches the topper to smaller still, to give even borders between each layer. Attach both with double-sided tape.

3 Cut out the topper and attach it to a piece of white card that is just a little bigger, then attach to the main card using double-sided tape.

4 Fix the ribbon and rose to the top left of the card using silicone glue.

Paper Roses

*The beautiful hat in this card is embellished with paper roses and
displayed against a darker background chosen from the same CD.*

Victorian Child

Materials:

- A4 sheet of brown card
- A5 sheet of coffee country lace backing paper
- A5 sheet of gold pearl card
- Sepia photograph
- Chocolate organza ribbon
- 5mm ($^3/_{16}$in) calligraphy gold felt tip pen

Tools:

- Bone folder
- Double-sided tape
- Guillotine
- 2mm ($^1/_8$in) foam tape
- Tweezers
- Decoupage snips

Instructions:

1 Fold the A4 sheet of brown card in half and crease heavily with a bone folder. Alternatively use a scoring board to fold the card. Then trim down to a square on the guillotine.

2 Cut the coffee lace paper down to a smaller size and using the decoupage snips (or a small pair of scissors), follow the line of the lace to get a wavy edge to one side.

3 Attach the coffee lace to the gold card with double-sided tape and then attach the gold card to the main brown card using foam tape to add a little lift to the card.

4 Drag the gold pen around the edge of the photograph to add a little gold line, then attach the photograph to the card using foam tape.

5 Finally tie the chocolate ribbon along the spine of the card and fix in a bow.

Rosy Girl

*Here the same photograph is given a more feminine look
with pink roses and pretty gold corner craft stickers.*

Sailor Boy

Materials:

A4 sheet of brown card

A5 sheet each of two designs of calligraphy backing paper

A5 piece of gold mirror card

5mm (³/₁₆in) calligraphy gold felt tip pen

Two sailor photographs

Tools:

Bone folder

Double-sided tape

Guillotine

Tweezers

Instructions:

1 Fold the A4 sheet of brown card in half and crease heavily with a bone folder. Alternatively use a scoring board to fold the card.

2 Cut the first calligraphy paper down to a smaller size and attach to the main card with double-sided tape, leaving a brown border.

3 Cut the second calligraphy paper smaller still and layer on to gold card, leaving a narrow gold border. Attach to the main card with double-sided tape.

4 Swipe the gold pen along the edges of the photographs.

5 Attach the photographs to the card with double-sided tape, overlapping them slightly.

Seafaring Days
The photographs are displayed against a warm, earth-toned marble paper and some die-cut bows have been added.

Sweet Pea Fairy

Materials:

A4 sheet of cream card plus a small piece

Two A5 sheets of sweet pea backing paper

A5 sheet of olive green pearl card

A4 sheet of burgundy card

Sweet Pea Fairy Stamp

Selection of Sakura Stardust sparkly pens

Tools:

Bone folder

Double-sided tape

Guillotine

Tweezers

Instructions:

1 Fold the A4 sheet of cream card in half and crease heavily with a bone folder. Alternatively use a scoring board to fold the card.

2 Cut the sweet pea paper down to a smaller size and mount it on the main card. Cut a piece of burgundy card smaller still to leave a border, then cut a second piece of sweet pea paper smaller than the burgundy paper. Layer and attach both pieces, leaving a border round each.

3 Stamp the image of the sweet pea fairy on cream card and colour it using the sparkly pens. Once dry, trim round the image and mount it on to first burgundy and then olive green card.

4 Fix the finished topper on to the card using double-sided tape.

Lace Paper Fairy

This Sweet Pea Fairy is framed by pastel lace papers and the corners have been decorated with a paper punch.

Publisher's Note
If you would like more books on the techniques
shown, try the following:
Handmade Victorian Cards by Joanna Sheen,
Search Press Ltd, 2007

Acknowledgements
A big thank you to everyone at Search Press,
especially Sophie, and thanks as always to
Debbie, a fab photographer. Thanks also to all
the crafting friends who have inspired ideas and
been such fun to learn with.